TONY PAMELL

MIKE TIME

The Essential Guide to Managing Your Time, Discover Effective Time Management Strategies So You Can Stop Putting Things Off and Get More Stuff Done

Descrierea CIP a Bibliotecii Naţionale a României
TONY PAMELL
   MIKE TIME. The Essential Guide to Managing Your Time, Discover Effective Time Management Strategies So You Can Stop Putting Things Off and Get More Stuff Done / Tony Pamell. – Bucharest: Editura My Ebook, 2020
   ISBN

TONY PAMELL

MIKE TIME

The Essential Guide to Managing Your Time, Discover Effective Time Management Strategies So You Can Stop Putting Things Off and Get More Stuff Done

My Ebook Publishing House
Bucharest, 2020

TABLE OF CONTENTS

Introduction: Procrastination & the Root of the Problem 7

Why Do We Procrastinate? 8

We Never Have Enough Time 10

How This Book Works 11

The Easy Way & the Hard Way 12

Step 1: It All Starts With Settings Goals 13

Step 2: Make a Plan To Get You From A To B 19

What is a Plan? 20

Setting a Realistic Timeframe 21

How to Create a Plan 22

Creating Milestones 24

Step 3: Break Down Your Milestones 29

How to Break Down a Milestone 32

Hey, What about Procrastination & All the Rest? 33

Step 4: Eliminate Distractions 37

Start With Your Schedule 38

Making Your Goal Time a Priority 40

Eliminating Distractions.. 41

A Word about Distractions.. 42

Step 5: Feel The Fear But Do It Anyway 44

Why You Have Fears And What To Do About It............... 45

Step 6: Beat Procrastination In 5 Stages......................... 48

Stage One: Identify the Problem 49

Stage Two: Decide If It is Legitimate 50

Stage Three: Look at Your List of Reasons 50

Stage Four: Imagine Yourself at the End of Your Goal...... 51

Stage Five: Just Do it! 52

Don't Overextend Yourself.. 53

Step 7: Get And Stay Motivated 54

Putting It All Into Action – Your Game Plan................. 62

My Final Words.. 67

INTRODUCTION

PROCRASTINATION & THE ROOT
OF THE PROBLEM

It brings me much pleasure to bring your this book – *Never Say Later*.

If you have ever found yourself wondering why you haven't reached the success that you want for yourself, or why your life isn't how you have imagined it, the problem just might lie in procrastination and putting things off. In fact, if you are reading this book, the odds are pretty good that's the case.

Procrastination, distractions and putting off important tasks are at the root of most people's lack of success, and it is something that highly successful people don't suffer from. Don't get me wrong, even the most successful people in the world procrastinate occasionally and everyone obviously gets distracted sometimes, but highly successful people don't let it stand in the way of what they want. They find ways to overcome it.

At first, when you have made a habit of procrastination, it can seem like reaching goals and quitting your procrastinating ways is almost impossible, but the truth is, people overcome it every single day, and you and I are no different than they are. What you need most is a plan of action – a step-by-step guide that will show you exactly how to eliminate procrastination from your life once and for all, and teach you how to make a habit of getting things done right away.

Why Do We Procrastinate?

Sometimes, procrastination is based on fear. We don't do what we want to, or think that we should, because we are afraid of failure, afraid of how much work it will be or have other fears.

Consider an aspiring musician. He or she knows that in order to be as good as some of their favorite musicians, they need to put in an hour or two of practice every single day. They might start strong, practicing two or three hours a day for the first few days, but then they begin to see that they are nowhere near the level that they want to be (even though they are just beginning) and begin to fear that they will never get to that level and will instead have wasted half of their life practicing. This fear pervades their thoughts and eventually, practice time gets shorter or less frequent, and they stop practicing entirely.

In other cases, we procrastinate because we are simply feeling lazy. It is a lot of work to accomplish something great, and even though most of us want to do exactly that, the work seems insurmountable. You might have convinced yourself that doing X will result in Y, but just aren't taking the steps to do it. Laziness is almost never the *sole* reason that we don't accomplish our goals, but it does factor in.

We also procrastinate because there are plenty of small, fun tasks that can be done during the day. For example, if you wanted to write a novel, and you were planning to write 1000 words, you might do small tasks that seem more appealing instead – such as naming your characters, creating backstories for them, or drawing a diagram of the town that you are setting your novel in. This stuff does have its time, but its time is not when you have decided to write 1000 words on your novel. This guide will not only address this issue, but will show you how to solve it easily.

We Never Have Enough Time

 If a person were to actually do everything on their to- do list all at once, without any time for distractions, breaks or extra tasks, they would probably find that they could finish in as little as three or four hours, and then have the rest of the day to do what they want. However, we never seem to do that. We can stretch out a one-hour project into a four-hour one easily with a little procrastination and a lot of loose schedule management. This guide will also address this issue, and teach you how to plan effectively and stick to that plan.

How This Book Works

This book was designed as a step-by-step guide. There are seven main steps that you will be following, but each step will be broken up into smaller ones (a philosophy that you'll soon be implementing yourself) and be easily digestible, or able to be completed easily in a short period of time. This book was designed for you to begin at the beginning and to complete each step at your own pace.

This book was also designed as a framework rather than a book chock-full of tips on eliminating procrastination and managing your time better. It is likely that your head is full of tips on these things, as you have probably tried to solve this problem before now.

Obviously, simply giving you the information didn't work – and almost never works – so this book is different. This book will take you through the entire process of completing a single, large goal and removing all of the obstacles that usually stand in your way like poor time management and getting distracted by email, Facebook and other techno-distractions.

In other words, it will be up to you to use this framework for each of your goals. Once you understand the process and have worked your way through a single goal, you will have no difficulty doing it with the other goals in your life.

The Easy Way & the Hard Way

You know in movies how the villain always asks the hero whether he wants the easy way or the hard way? In other words, does the hero want to come quietly or does he want to fight his way through, taking more time and expending more energy. For some reason, the hero always chooses the hard way, but you don't have to do that here. In fact, once you understand this guide, you will find that achieving your goals is easy. In the past, you have always done exactly what that movie hero did – chose the hard way, but now I'm going to show you the easy way, and after reading this book, you'll wonder why you have been choosing the hard way for so long. Let's get started, because there is no time like the present.

Step 1: IT ALL STARTS WITH SETTINGS GOALS

Your first task in reaching your goal is to set one. That makes sense, right? But it isn't as simple as writing something down on a piece of paper. You need to make sure that you have a specific goal, one that has benchmarks and can actually be measured. We're going to use fitness as an example goal throughout most of this guide, so let's get started with setting our first fitness goal.

Goal: To get in shape

Good. You have a goal. But what does getting in shape mean? How do you know when you achieve it? What specific measureable results do you need to have to know that you are "in shape?" See what I mean about specifics. So, let's try setting that goal again.

Goal: To weigh 185 pounds

That's much better, much more specific and gives you an actual measurement that you can use when you have reached the goal. When you weigh 185 pounds, you'll know that you are in shape. But what if you have other goals along with the weight loss? What if you want to build muscle as well and be able to run 3 miles a day without any problems? So, we need to get more specific.

Goal: *To get in shape – meaning to weigh 185 pounds, have 20 inch biceps and be able to run a mile in less than 10 minutes*

That's much better. Now we have defined exactly what you want from your goal, but there is one problem still remaining. Can you spot it? Your goal doesn't leave any room for flexibility. For example, what if you simply can't have 20 inch biceps? If you have a very small frame, you not only might not be able to achieve that goal (or at least not achieve it for a very long time) but you might look extremely silly with biceps that large.

Also, since muscle is more dense than fat, it is very probable that you can weigh 200 or even 225 pounds and still be in shape, maybe in the best shape of your life. So, you need to allow for a little flexibility in the goal.

This might not seem important, but in fact, it is vital. When you start the long journey to achieving your goal, your mind will be looking for any and every excuse to stop. If you subconsciously realize that you aren't going to be able to have 20 inch biceps, your mind will have a very easy time talking you out of working out. So, let's try setting that goal one last time.

Goal: To get in shape.

Benchmark   1:   Weigh between 185 and 225 pounds

Benchmark   2:   Biceps 17-20 inches

Benchmark   3:   Run a mile within 9 minutes, or 3 miles within 30 minutes.

Benchmark   4:   Feel fit, trim and in shape.

See how much more clearly you can see the end result of that goal, and how much better you feel knowing that you don't necessarily have to waste away to 185 pounds before you reach it. The main objective is to give yourself a target to shoot for, and you don't need the target to be the tiny bullseye in the very center of the target. You just need to be within the inner rings.

Just in case fitness isn't your goal, let's try this method out with a few other sample goals. Many people have the goal of becoming rich, or at the very least, financially independent. However, you might want to work on making more money rather than vague terms like "rich" and "financially independent." Making more money is something that you can set benchmarks for.

Goal: To make more money

Benchmark 1:   Have an income of at least $100,000 per year.

Benchmark 2:   To have total debt (not including mortgage) of less than $1000.

Benchmark 3:   To work 30 hours a week or less.

So, in this example, you have some clearly defined financial goals. You want to increase your income, but you don't want to work more hours than you already do. This is a great end goal to have, because it clearly defines what you want and gives you a definite set of goals. You might have to work more than 30 hours while you are reaching the goal, but your goal isn't to work 30 hours per week while you are on your way to financial freedom, it is to eventually get there, and that is an important distinction.

Let's do another.

Suppose that you have a goal that is difficult to define, like being less awkward in social situations. You can still make benchmarks that you can use to measure your success. For example:

Goal: To improve social skills

Benchmark 1: Have at least 15 people that you consider a friend, and consider you a friend.

Benchmark 2: Get at least 1 phone number from a member of the opposite sex when you go out.

Benchmark 3: Feel comfortable in a group of people.

Now, bear in mind that you don't need exactly three benchmarks, although you should have at least two, and you probably shouldn't have more than six or seven because it will discourage you knowing that you have to reach those requirements before you can call your goal completed.

Also, it is important to keep in mind that you don't have to show your goals to anyone. You can be as specific and bare your heart completely, because no one has to see your goals. There will be no teacher at the end of this book showing up, demanding to see your goals.

So, let's get started with the first step. Write down a goal that you want to achieve and include 2-7 benchmarks with it that will help you know when you reach that goal. Take some time and think about it. This book was designed to work at your pace, so take as much time as you want and come back to the next chapter when you have a goal, clearly defined benchmarks and are ready to learn how to proceed to achieve it.

Step 2: MAKE A PLAN TO GET YOU FROM A TO B

Your second step in reaching your goals and eliminating distractions and procrastination from your life is making a plan. If you are like most motivated people, you have probably made a plan before. In fact, you have probably made dozens of plans, each of them as doomed to fail as the previous one. Why? Because you haven't yet learned the mechanics of making a good plan that will always succeed.

What is a Plan?

A plan is simply a way for you to get from point A to point B. You wouldn't think of traveling across an unfamiliar part of the country without a map, would you? A plan is your map to reaching your destination – the goal that you have set for yourself and likely the bigger that the goal is, the more detailed that your plan will have to be. Plans can be as simple as a goal and an instruction for achieving it, or as complex as a whole list of instructions and times to perform them, but the type of plan that you want to make is one that gives you a path and set of milestones on the way to your plan. You already have your end benchmarks, which means that you'll know when you actually arrive at your destination, but just like road signs when traveling along the interstate, you'll want milestones along the way that tell you that you are on your way to achieving your goals, and that you are on track with whatever time frame that you have set.

Setting a Realistic Timeframe

The timeframe is exactly the next subject that we'll cover. Timeframe is something that many people struggle with because they often don't give themselves enough time to achieve their goals, which causes instant frustration.

Your subconscious mind is much smarter than your conscious one. It knows that you aren't going to lose 100 pounds in six months. The only way that it is likely to happen is if you put everything in your life on hold and spent 8-10 hours a day in the gym, working out, and eating just a few hundred calories a day. Not only is that extremely unhealthy, it is usually impossible.

A smaller majority of people give themselves too much time to achieve their goals, and that causes a different problem. This creates apathy and laziness. You want to pay off $10,000 worth of debt in the next 20 years?

That is perfectly achievable but it leaves a lot of room for getting into debt and getting out again. In other words, it removes the immediacy from the goal. So, you need to find a balanced timeframe that isn't too long, but definitely isn't too short.

How to Create a Plan

Your plan isn't a daily list of activities that will allow you to reach your goals, although that is something that many people do when they first set a goal. A plan, as previously mentioned, is a set of milestones that will help you determine where you are and whether you are on track, as well as a map that tells you how to get to that end result of achieving your goal with the benchmarks included. So, let's use the fitness example that was mentioned earlier to create a good, solid plan.

Remember this from chapter one?

Goal: To get in shape.

Benchmark 1: Weigh between 185 and 225 pounds

Benchmark 2: Biceps 17-20 inches

Benchmark 3: Run a mile within 9 minutes, or 3 miles within 30 minutes.

Benchmark 4: Feel fit, trim and in shape.

So, to create a plan based upon this goal and the benchmarks, we need to start with a timeframe. The timeframe that it takes to achieve this goal will vary based upon where you are starting from. If you weigh 250 pounds and are in reasonable shape, this goal might only take 3-6 months, but if you are 400 pounds and have never been inside a gym, you might want to set your timeframe for 3-5 years or whatever realistic time period works for you.

You'll have to do a little research to determine what a realistic timeframe is for whatever goal you have in mind. If you can't nail down a solid timeframe, don't worry. Just come up with a general timeframe and mark it as "pending." You'll have a much clearer picture on how long it will take once we create your milestones.

In the case of our example, we're going to start with a timeframe of two years. So, here is what our plan looks like so far.

Goal: To get in shape.

Benchmark 1: Weigh between 185 and 225 pounds

Benchmark 2: Biceps 17-20 inches

Benchmark 3: Run a mile within 9 minutes, or 3 miles within 30 minutes.

Benchmark 4: Feel fit, trim and in shape.

Timeframe: 2 Years (December 31st, 2016)

Creating Milestones

 If we use the fitness example that we have been using all along, we can easily create milestones along the way. Milestones are creating using periods of time, and the ones that you will use depend entirely upon what your timeframe is. In the case of our example, we are going to create 12 milestones of two months each.

Assuming our starting time is January 1st, 2015, here is what our milestone structure will look like.

Milestone 1 (Feb 28th, 2015):

Milestone 2: (Apr 30th, 2015):

Milestone 3: (June 30th, 2015):

Milestone 4: (Aug 31st, 2015):

Milestone 5: (Oct 31st, 2015):

Milestone 6: (Dec 31st, 2015):

Milestone 7: (Feb 29th, 2016):

Milestone 8: (Apr 30th, 2016):

Milestone 9: (June 30th, 2016):

Milestone 10: (Aug 31st, 2016):

Milestone 11: (Oct 31st, 2016):

Milestone 12: (Dec 31st, 2016):

Now you have the beginnings of a good plan that you can easily track throughout your progression. Of course, you next need to fill in your milestones with realistic expectations for each. For example:

Goal: To get in shape.

Benchmark 1: Weigh between 185 and 225 pounds

Benchmark 2: Biceps 17-20 inches

Benchmark 3: Run a mile within 9 minutes, or 3 miles within 30 minutes.

Benchmark 4: Feel fit, trim and in shape. *Timeframe: 2 Years (December 31st, 2016)*

MILESTONES

Milestone 1 (Feb 28th, 2015): Lose 10 Pounds (320), Biceps 14 inches, 20 minute mile

Milestone 2: (Apr 30th, 2015): Lose 10 Pounds (310), Biceps 14.5 inches, 19 minute mile

Milestone 3: (June 30th, 2015): Lose 10 Pounds (300), Biceps 15 inches, 18 minute mile

Milestone 4: (Aug 31st, 2015): Lose 10 Pounds (290), Biceps 15.5 inches, 17 minute mile

Milestone 5: (Oct 31st, 2015): Lose 10 Pounds (280), Biceps 16 inches, 16 minute mile

Milestone 6: (Dec 31st, Biceps 16.5 inches, 152015): Lose 10 minute mile

Milestone 7: (Feb 29th, 2016): Lose 10 Pounds (260), Biceps 17 inches, 14 minute mile

Milestone 8: (Apr 30th, 2016): Lose 10 Pounds (250), Biceps 17.5 inches, 13 Minute mile

Milestone 9: (June 30th, 2016): Lose 10 Pounds (240), Biceps 18 inches, 12 minute mile

Milestone 10: (Aug 31st, 2016): Lose 10 Pounds (230), Biceps 18.5 inches, 11 minute mile

Milestone 11: (Oct 31st, 2016): Lose 10 Pounds (220), Biceps 19 inches, 10 minute mile

Milestone 12: (Dec 31st, 2016): Lose 10 Pounds (210), Biceps 20 inches, 9 minute mile

Okay, pay attention because this is important. *These milestones are not set in stone.* You're going to change them later. That's right – we're adding in the all-important flexibility. You may not reach your goal of 14 inches after just two months. You may have to spend some time learning how to work out first. You might also exceed your goal within the first two months on any of the milestones. Every time you reach a milestone, figure out your milestone benchmarks and reset your milestones accordingly.

This is an extremely important step, because if you only lose 5 pounds the first two months instead of ten, your mind is going to try to make you quit if you simply add the 5 pounds to the next milestone (for a total of 15 pounds in two months). Also, particularly with losing weight, you are likely going to lose a lot of weight in the beginning and a little bit at the end. That's because the more you weight, the higher your metabolism (don't believe the myth that heavy people have slower metabolisms than skinny people. It just isn't true). You must adjust your milestones every time you reach one. You won't be able to reach your goal otherwise.

So, now that we have our goal, our benchmarks at the end and our milestones, each with their own benchmarks, we can proceed with Step Three – breaking down a milestone. Whenever you have your milestones completed, move onto the next chapter.

Step 3: BREAK DOWN YOUR MILESTONES

We already know a fair bit about the imaginary person that is going to be using our sample plan, so we may as well name him. We know that Robert (our imaginary person) is 310 pounds, has 13 inch biceps currently and can run a mile in just over 20 minutes. We also know that his goal is to get in shape. Let's take another look at Robert's plan before we move onto how to break down a milestone.

Robert's Plan

Goal: To get in shape.

Benchmark 1: Weigh between 185 and 225 pounds

Benchmark 2: Biceps 17-20 inches

Benchmark 3: Run a mile within 9 minutes, or 3 miles within 30 minutes.

Benchmark 4: Feel fit, trim and in shape.

Timeframe: 2 Years (December 31st, 2016)

MILESTONES

Milestone 1 (Feb 28th, 2015): Lose 10 Pounds (320), Biceps 14 inches, 20 minute mile

Milestone 2: (Apr 30th, 2015): Lose 10 Pounds (310), Biceps 14.5 inches, 19 minute mile

Milestone 3: (June 30th, 2015): Lose 10 Pounds (300), Biceps 15 inches, 18 minute mile

Milestone 4: (Aug 31st, 2015): Lose 10 Pounds (290), Biceps 15.5 inches, 17 minute mile

Milestone 5: (Oct 31st, 2015): Lose 10 Pounds (280), Biceps 16 inches, 16 minute mile

Milestone 6: (Dec 31st, 2015): Lose 10 Pounds (270), Biceps 16.5 inches, 15 minute mile

Milestone 7: (Feb 29th, 2016): Lose 10 Pounds (260), Biceps 17 inches, 14 minute mile

Milestone 8: (Apr 30th, 2016): Lose 10 Pounds (250), Biceps 17.5 inches, 13 minute mile

Milestone 9: (June 30th, 2016): Lose 10 Pounds (240), Biceps 18   inches, 12 minute mile

Milestone 10: (Aug 31st, 2016): Lose 10 Pounds (230), Biceps 18.5 inches, 11 minute mile

Milestone 11: (Oct 31st, 2016): Lose 10 Pounds (220), Biceps 19 inches, 10 minute mile

Milestone 12: (Dec 31st, 2016): Lose 10 Pounds (210), Biceps 20 inches, 9 minute mile

How to Break Down a Milestone

You still should only have a general idea of how to get to your end goal if you have followed along so far. But that's why we're going to break down your first milestone. Here is another important tip. Don't break down any other milestone except your first. Why is that? Everyone in unison now: *because your milestones are going to change.* Good. Now, let's break down Robert's first milestone.

Milestone 1 (Feb 28th, 2015): Lose 10 Pounds (320), Biceps 14 inches, 20 minute mile

In order to achieve these benchmarks (and you should only be concentrating on these benchmarks) you need to decide what you need to do, and how often you need to do it. Now, before we get so mired in Robert's goals that we forget out yours, keep in mind that it doesn't matter if your goal is to write a novel, play, get in shape, start a business or achieve financial freedom another way, it is all the same. We need to break down a milestone to know exactly what we have to do.

Hey, What about Procrastination & All the Rest?

You might be wondering when the information comes about procrastination and eliminating distractions. Be patient, because unless you have a clearly defined plan-of-action, eliminating all of the distractions in the world and never procrastinating ever again will get you exactly nowhere.

As mentioned, unless you have a map to get you to your goal, you have no chance of reaching it, even if you are locked in a room with no television, phone or computer and have zero to do but work on it. Unless you have a goal, with clearly defined tasks to reach it, eliminating those things won't help. But not to worry, that information is coming.

Let's get back to breaking down a milestone. Robert's milestone is below. He wants to lose 10 pounds, have 14 inch biceps and run a 20 minute mile.

Assuming that Robert is 330 pounds, has 13 inch biceps and runs a mile in about 25 minutes, this goal is perfectly achievable in two months.

Milestone 1 (Feb 28th, 2015): Lose 10 Pounds (320), Biceps 14 inches, 20 minute mile

You will break down your milestone using one benchmark at a time. If you want to lose 10 pounds, you will need to break down your milestone into even smaller steps. You know that there are 8 weeks in two months, so let's take Robert's goal of losing 10 pounds and break it down for those 8 weeks. That's 1.25 pounds per week.

Now, in order to reach his goal of adding an inch to his biceps by the first milestone he will need to break it down for 8 weeks. This one is easy. He just needs to add 1/8 of an inch per week to his bicep.

Finally, he wants to run a mile in 20 minutes. Currently, he can run a mile in 25 minutes. That means for Robert's milestone, he needs to eliminate about 40 seconds from his time every week. So, here is what a breakdown of Robert's first milestone will look like.

Milestone 1 (Feb 28th, 2015): Lose 10 Pounds (320), Biceps 14 inches, 20 minute mile

Week 1: Lose 1.25 Pounds, Add 1/8" to biceps, Run mile in 24:20

Week 2: Lose 1.25 Pounds, Add 1/8" to biceps, Run mile in 23:40

Week 3: Lose 1.25 Pounds, Add 1/8" to biceps, Run mile in 23:00

Week 4: Lose 1.25 Pounds, Add 1/8" to biceps, Run mile in 22:20

Week 5: Lose 1.25 Pounds, Add 1/8" to biceps, Run mile in 21:40

Week 6: Lose 1.25 Pounds, Add 1/8" to biceps, Run mile in 21:00

Week 7: Lose 1.25 Pounds, Add 1/8" to biceps, Run mile in 20:30

Week 8: Lose 1.25 Pounds, Add 1/8" to biceps, Run mile in 20:00

See how easy Robert's goals have become once they have been broken down into smaller steps, ones that are easily achievable. Now, all Robert (and you) has to do is decide what it would take to achieve these little goals. Losing a pound and a quarter means that Robert is going to have to burn 4375 more calories than he eats, or 625 calories per day. Adding an 1/8th of an inch to his biceps will probably require doing bicep exercises two or three times a week, and running a mile will require at least three runs per week, each one slightly faster than the last.

Now, Robert has all of the information that he needs to reach his goal – concentrating mostly on just the first milestone mind you. You can do the same thing. Break down your first milestone and decide what you need to do daily or weekly in order to reach it. Once you have that list you are ready to proceed with eliminating the distractions, the procrastination and the putting-off habits that you have that will keep you from achieving it. Setting your goals and creating your milestones is just the first step. You actually need to do the tasks that you have set for yourself, and that's what the next few chapters are about.

Step 4: ELIMINATE DISTRACTIONS

Distractions are all around us. Most of us have our phones, which are our lifelines to the time-sucking (but addictive) websites like Facebook, Twitter, Instagram and Email. Besides these techno-distractions, we also have our spouse, vying for our attention, our children, our extended family members, all who want a piece of our time, plus our friends want to see us once in a while. Add to all that the 40-50 hours per week that you spend at work and it is easy to see why we don't have time to achieve our goals – or at least why we *think* we don't have the time. So, how do you solve these problems?

Start With Your Schedule

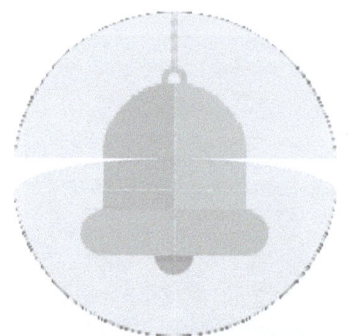

You might already have a schedule, but it is likely that you don't include most of what you do during the day on it.

For example, you might know that you have to be up at 6 am to make breakfast and get the kids off to school, and be to work by 8am, but what I want you to do is make a schedule for literally everything that you do. You have a lot of people vying for your attention and time, but if you schedule the time for them, you will find that you have plenty of space to achieve your goals.

Let's go back to Robert and his goals.

Robert somehow needs to find time to run a mile a few times a week, work out at the gym and watch what he eats.

Robert is a typical American, as many of the people reading this book are bound to be, and has a wife, children, friends, a full-time job and other obligations. But Robert simply needs to move some things around to make time for his goals. This isn't always easy, but it is achievable.

For example, since Robert works Monday – Friday, he could run on Wednesday evenings, and then on Saturday and Sunday. That should allow him to be able to shave off that 40 seconds that he needs to achieve his weekly goal by the end of the week. Robert also needs to cut down on his calories, or burn more through exercise. All Robert has to do is cut down on his food intake by about 625 calories a day, which is as simple as eliminating one Big Mac & small fries from his diet, or trading in that morning White Chocolate Mocha Latte for a cup of black coffee instead. As for the gym, Robert needs about 45 minutes, three times a week, to achieve his goal. So, if he can find 45 minutes on Monday, Thursday and

Saturday evenings to work out for 45 minutes (even better if he has a home gym) and run a mile on Wednesday evenings and sometime on Saturday and Sunday, Robert will be able to achieve his goal.

You also can achieve your goal by doing the same thing. Figure out how much time you need to devote to your goals and make time for them.

Squeeze them in however you can, but *make them a priority*. Then, I'll explain how to eliminate the distractions of Facebook, Twitter, kids, friends and other obligations to make sure that you achieve your weekly goals.

Making Your Goal Time a Priority

If you know that if you don't pay that traffic ticket by the end of this week, the fine will double; you will probably find the time to pay it, won't you?

Even if you have to go down to the courthouse and stand in line for two hours to pay the ticket, you would still find the time to pay it somehow. Your goals should be even a higher priority. While you may not always be able to work on them at the same time every day or week, *they must be completed.* Say it with me: **They must be completed**.

I suggest making a weekly checklist of what you need to do to achieve that week's goals and hanging it somewhere where you'll have to walk past it often, even if that means directly over the toilet in your bathroom. As you complete each item, check it off and make sure that everything is checked by the end of the week.

Eliminating Distractions

We're going to take all of the time-sucking distractions and find out exactly how you can eliminate them from your goal time. Remember, your goal time is sacred. The check list must be completed, and that means that distractions are *not allowed* during goal time.

Facebook, Twitter & Social Media: This one is easy. Don't bring your phone to goal time. You can use it whenever you aren't working on your goals, but during goals time, your phone is not allowed.

Neither is your tablet or matches and kindling (in case you want to tweet smoke signals). Nothing is allowed to interfere with goal time. Period. Obviously, I'm not going to add your computer and internet access to this list, because you may need it for whatever goal you are trying to achieve, but social media is not allowed during goal time (unless it is directly related to

41

your goal). The only thing that you are allowed to do during goal time is complete what is on your checklist.

Kids/Spouse/Friends: Let everyone know that you are going to be doing X on Day Y and Z and that you cannot be bothered during that time. Lock the door if you have to, or complete the item on your checklist out of the house and away from everyone.

Other Obligations: You have church or charity board meetings? You have been asked to be a speaker at the Rotary Club? If it interferes with goal time then cancel it. You need to make sure that you make goal time and completing that weekly checklist one of your top priorities.

A Word about Distractions

In another book, you might have found this entire chapter devoted on means to disconnect yourself from the digital world using website blocking software or some other means to keep you from using social media or watching YouTube videos. However, as I mentioned at the beginning of this book, this plan is different than what you might be used to. I'm not going to fill this book up with suggestions on how to eliminate distractions and overcome procrastination unless it directly relates to your goal time.

The reason that most people fail at achieving their goals is not because they need to eliminate Twitter, Facebook and the internet in general from their life – it is because they don't understand how little time it really takes to achieve their goals. Anyone can stay off Twitter and Facebook and avoid family obligations for the however many hours a week that it takes to achieve a goal, as long as they understand that goal time is one of their main priorities.

In the next chapter, we'll talk about how to deal with fears that might prevent you from completing your checklist.

Step 5: FEEL THE FEAR BUT DO IT ANYWAY

If I have made achieving goals sound easy, then I apologize. It isn't as difficult as most people think, but it also isn't easy. The main reason that it is difficult, even if you break it into small chunks like I have suggested is that you're going to be overwhelmed with fears when you first start, and pretty much every step along the way, although it does get easier the longer that you have been working on a goal.

Why You Have Fears And What To Do About It

Humans are natural fear-mongers. We are fearful about everything, and it extends to just about every part of our life. We're fearful about our homes being robbed so we lock our doors. We're fearful about someone picking the lock, so we buy a dog. We're fearful about the dog not reacting when someone tries to break in so we get an expensive alarm system. Most importantly, as it relates to our topic, we're fearful that we're not going to reach our goals – or even worse – that we won't be happy once we do.

Fear can hold us back from achieving our goals, and it can be the number one factor for our lack of success. Fear doesn't just manifest itself once and then disappear either; it comes in a vicious cycle that keeps you from success. For example, let's go back to Robert and his goal of getting in shape. Reasons vary why someone would want to get in shape. Some people just want to be healthy and live longer, others are doing it for the chicks/dudes (a perfectly acceptable reason believe it or not) and some have serious reasons for doing it like a heart condition, diabetes or they want to become an actor or recording artist and want to be fit and trim to do it.

Robert's reason – since he's imaginary I'm imagining – is that he wants to be healthy and live longer. But the first time that Robert heads out to the track to run his 24 minute mile the fears will start plaguing him. What if this doesn't work? You've been overweight your whole life, what makes you think that anything will change now? You're too old to get in shape. You could lose weight and get healthy and then get run over by a truck, so why not enjoy life?

All of this self-talk that Robert is having (which will very likely be similar to the self-talk that you will have) is based in fear. All of it. And Robert has been letting fear keep him from losing weight his entire life. He starts having these fears, and they start changing his mind about his goals. There is only one thing that you can do with these fears. *Ignore them.*

They aren't going to go away. They aren't going to stop trying to get you to quit going after your dreams. Fears will always exist, and the best way to deal with them is simply to ignore them.

The first step in learning to do so is being honest with yourself. You know that the lies that your fears are trying to tell you are just that – lies. But you want to believe them so that you don't have to put forth the effort required for change. Don't feel bad – it's all part of the human condition and all of us do it. But try to look past those fears when they pop up and truly ask yourself if any of the things that the fears are telling you are likely to be true. Then, ask yourself if you would want to accomplish the goal even if it did turn out to be the truth. You'll find that the answer will always be yes – you would.

If you are struggling with fears, the best way to overcome them truly is by ignoring them and doing it anyway. Once you have accomplished a few of your checklists, and have reached a milestone or two, you'll notice that while the fears do not actually go away, they do get quite a bit less persistent and quieter.

If you are serious about your goals, you'll complete them anyway, even in the presence of fear, and eventually, overcoming those little voices in your head that we all have will be as easy as tuning out low music or muted voices from the neighbors in the next apartment. You will have overcome fear. Now, let's deal with procrastination.

Step 6: BEAT PROCRASTINATION IN 5 STAGES

Overcoming procrastination isn't going to be easy. If you are like most people who have struggled to reach their goals, you have probably made a habit out of procrastination. It is difficult to break a habit but it can be done. The first step is obviously making sure that you are aware of what is expected of you – what you expect of yourself – and that means putting your goal checklist for the week in a place that you will constantly see it.

As previously mentioned, I suggest putting it right over the toilet, or on the bathroom door, so that every time you come into the bathroom you will see it and be reminded of what you need to do that week. However, as the week continues, you will almost certainly find yourself coming up with reasons why you don't need to complete the items on the checklist today – even if you have the time. That can be deadly to your plan, because everything rides on you taking those small steps to reach your goals. Here is another (surprise!) step-by-step checklist that will allow you to overcome procrastination when it crops up.

Stage One: Identify the Problem

You're likely not just procrastinating out of laziness, but even if you are, you need to identify the problem. If you look at your list, and you realize that you could spend the next thirty minutes completing one of the items on it, but you don't want to do it, or want to put it off until tomorrow, you need to identify why you are feeling that way. It could be that those fears that we discussed in the previous chapter are cropping up. It could be that you simply don't remember why you made your goals, benchmarks, milestones and weekly goals in the first place. Or it could be that you just happen to be feeling lazy that day. You might even have a legitimate reason for not doing it. For example, you don't want to go on a mile run because you only have 30 minutes before you have to be back to work and you need to shower after you run a mile. No matter what the case, you need to identify why it is that you want to put off completing a checklist item until tomorrow and then we can decide what to do with it.

Stage Two: Decide If It is Legitimate

If you have a legitimate reason for not completing the task right now, then it's fine to put it off until tomorrow. If you don't, then you can move onto the next step in overcoming procrastination.

Stage Three: Look at Your List of Reasons

This does not mean that you should procrastinate further by making a list of reasons why you want to accomplish your end goal. You should make this list at the same time that you are making your goal or goals and breaking them down as instructed earlier. If you find yourself putting off your tasks then you should look at your list so that you can get jazzed up once again about accomplishing your goal. We'll go over some more specific motivational techniques in the next chapter.

Stage Four: Imagine Yourself at the End of Your Goal

If reviewing your list didn't do the trick and you still find yourself thinking about skipping your goal checklist for the day, then take a few seconds and imagine yourself at the end of your goal if you complete it. If your goal is to become financially independent and work 20 hours a week, then imagine yourself sitting on your couch, knowing that your four hours of work are done for the day and you can do anything you want with the rest of your time. If your goal is weight loss or fitness, imagine yourself thin, fit and looking great. Imagine yourself out on the town, garnering looks from the opposite sex.

Now, spend a few more seconds thinking about what it would be like if you didn't accomplish your goal. Imagine that you are two years older and you are still in the same financial state that you are now, or you are in even more debt and are making less money than you are right now. If you are concentrating on weight loss, imagine that you don't lose a single pound over the next few years. Imagine the looks that you'll be getting then, and how different they will be from what you'll get if you actually accomplish your goal. Then, imagine if you gained even more weight, another 100 pounds for example.

When you finish with these visualization techniques, you should be able to overcome procrastination even of the most stubborn variety. If not, go ahead and go onto step five.

Stage Five: Just Do it!

If you have reached this point and you are still trying to put off doing whatever it is on your weekly checklist that you have time to do, and can't find a legitimate reason for not doing, just do the damned thing anyway!

You have made this a goal, and even though you have failed at it before, you don't have to fail this time. You can make this happen. You don't need to be stuck in that financial rut forever, nor do you need to be overweight and out of shape. Whatever your goal happens to be, just go ahead and do the task. You'll feel better after you accomplish it and put a big checkmark through the box next to it.

Don't Overextend Yourself

It is important that you don't try to accomplish too many goals at the same time, because if you do, your procrastination on accomplishing some of them will come from simple exhaustion. You can probably find the time to accomplish two or three goals at the same time, depending upon what kind of goals they are and the work that goes into them. Some goals you may have to do by themselves, but any more than two or three goals usually means that you not only don't have enough time to accomplish the weekly goals that will get you to the end of your milestones, it also means that you're exhausted about halfway through the week. Make sure that your procrastination doesn't come from having too many goals at once, and if that is the case, just remove one or two of them to complete at a later date.

Now, let's move onto the seventh and final step in this guide, which will be give you some great ways to create motivation and stay motivated throughout your entire journey reaching your goals, and not only that, but enjoy the journey.

Step 7: GET AND STAY MOTIVATED

You have arrived at the final step of this guide – creating the motivation that you'll need to keep going throughout your goal journey. You're going to need as much motivation as you can, and so this chapter will be structured a little differently.

Rather than go through a step-by-step to keeping motivated or discussing it, I'm going to list some great ways that I have found (through my own goal-setting and goal-reaching efforts as well as through research) to keep motivated for months or years at a time. I strongly suggest that you use at least a few of these as you begin your journey and you may end up using them all by the time that you are done.

Track Your Progress Visually: While you already have what you want to achieve down on paper (even if your paper is your computer) you also want to put down what you have accomplished up to this point. Then, you want to print it out and put it somewhere that you will see it every single day.

When you are feeling less motivated than normal you will look at everything that you have accomplished so far towards your goal or goals and you may feel that motivational spurt once again. A giant poster board showing your progress with colorful magic markers does a great job of this.

Don't Get Ahead of Yourself: This is especially true with exercise but the principle applies with any goal. You might feel that you can accomplish anything when you first start, and that could cause you to overextend yourself and get burned out. Resist the temptation and hold back, and only accomplish what is on your goal checklist. That's exactly why we broke it down into little tiny chunks the way we did.

Join a Group: If you are focusing on weight loss, there is a great website called MyFitnessPal that is not only a way to track your calories and exercise and help you achieve your goals of X pounds per week, but it also is a very social site, allowing your friends to see your progress and help encourage you. Depending upon your specific goal, there may be groups on the internet that you can join as well as forums and Facebook Groups. There may even be meet-ups in real life that you can join and attend to stay motivated. Check out Meetup.com to find meetup groups around your area.

Post Pictures of Your Goal: This will be different depending upon what your goal is, but you should be able to find pictures for just about anything.

If your goal is financial freedom, then post Photoshop pictures of your bank balance being in the hundreds of thousands of dollars range, or a picture of your dream car, boat or home. If your goal is weight loss, post a picture of someone that you want to look like. Post them somewhere where you are sure to see them all the time like your wall, on your desk or even as your computer background.

NOTE: This does not work the opposite way. If you post pictures of yourself overweight or a picture of your bank balance hovering around zero you are going to be thinking negative and you always want to stay positive about your goals.

Set up a Reward System: Remember creating milestones for your goals, and weekly checklists? We did that for several reasons, not just because smaller tasks are easier to manage. We break up our goals into smaller tasks because first, you will feel good about even accomplishing a weekly checklist or one milestone, and two, so that you can reward yourself when you reach those points. Set up a reward system for your checklists, and create larger rewards for your milestones.

Get Someone to Partner with You: If you are trying to lose weight, quit smoking or any other goal that you can partner up with someone on, you definitely should. Not every goal will be able to make this work but many of them are perfectly suited for a "goal buddy." You will find that you will motivate each other just by knowing that you are on the same path. This works even better if you can add in some friendly competition – such as (with weight loss) weighing in on a weekly basis Biggest Loser style.

Make Completing Checklist Items Pleasurable: A great way to do this is make a playlist of your favorite songs, and only listen to them while you are completing checklist items. This works extremely well for exercise and weight loss, but it can also work while you are on the computer working on financial freedom. You don't necessarily have to use music, but you should try to make accomplishing checklist items as pleasantly as you can.

Find a Coach or Mentor: Find someone that you know who has already had success in accomplishing the same goal or a similar goal and meet with them once a week to review your progress. Not only will you be more motivated knowing that you have someone that you have to answer to, but you will also gain valuable insight into reaching your goals by finding out about their own experiences in reaching theirs.

Review Your Reason List Often: Remember the reason list that we discussed earlier in the chapter on procrastination? You don't have to wait until you are procrastinating something in order to review it. In fact, you should review it regularly – daily if you can find the time. An even better solution is to hang it on the wall right next to your checklist for the week so that whenever you look at your checklist and consider doing something on that list and marking it off, you can glance over at your list of reasons and remember why you're doing it in the first place.

Create or Find Inspiration Daily: There are many ways that you can create inspiration. You can write down a new reason for accomplishing your goal each day, or you can write down something that will change about your life if you have accomplished your goal. For example, if you are after financial freedom, you can write down a list of things that you won't have to worry about once you have enough money and time to do what you want, or a list of things that you'll be able to buy once you are making the kind of money that you want. If you are doing fitness goals, you might write down a list of ways that your life will change every single day once you have reached your goal. If you cannot think of a way to create inspiration, consider buying one of those calendars that give you inspiration daily, or have something inspirational sent to your inbox every day.

Make a Rule - Never Procrastinate More Than Once Per Week: If you make it an unbreakable rule that you will not procrastinate more than once per week, odds are that you will procrastinate exactly once, and the rest of the week you will accomplish what is on your checklist NOTE: Do not allow your "free procrastinations" to roll over to another week, and then save them up for a week of accomplishing nothing. You will have a really tough time getting motivated once that week is up.

Maintain a Journal: A journal of your thoughts and ideas while you are accomplishing your goals can help you to stay motivated. If you find yourself becoming discouraged a few milestones from now, simply look back through your journal and see how far you have come. This is the same sort of idea as putting up a visual representation of your progress, but a journal can be much more effective, because it can include how you're feeling and how you have overcome fears or procrastination when these things have cropped up.

Announce Your Goals to the World: This doesn't necessarily mean that you need to do exactly what I said earlier that you wouldn't have to do – show your goals to someone. It just means that whatever goals you feel comfortable sharing, share them with everyone you can. Your immediate and extended family is a good start, but it can be even more effective with strangers, which is why starting a blog or a YouTube channel can be a great motivator for you. Even better, you will be motivating others with your progress and that can keep you going for months or years down the road.

Think Positive Thoughts Daily: You want to make sure that each day you wake up; you think positive thoughts about your goals. Negative self-talk will get you in a negative state of mind and you'll start letting fears, procrastination and distractions keep you from your weekly checklists.

Don't allow negativity in. Always think positive, even when you feel discouraged.

PUTTING IT ALL INTO ACTION –
YOUR GAME PLAN

If you have made it this far, you should already have your goals, milestones and the rest, but in case you decided to read the entire book before beginning, this chapter will be a review of everything that we've gone over so far so that you can easily make your plan from here. Obviously, not everything can be covered in a review chapter, or it would be as long as the rest of the book, but we'll try to go over the basics.

Step 1: It All Starts With Setting Goals

Set the first goal that you want to accomplish. Obviously, you'll do this with every goal that you want to accomplish, but you don't want to overload yourself, so I suggest starting with one or two to begin with. Once you have your goal written down, create at least two, but no more than six or seven benchmarks that will allow you to know when you have reached your goal. If you need more information, revisit chapter one.

Step 2: Make a Plan To Get You From A To B

First, create a tentative time-frame for reaching your goal, and achieving all of your benchmarks. You may change this after you have finished mapping out your milestones, which is the next step. Divide up your timeframe into milestones and create a progress benchmark for each of your main benchmarks. So, if your goal time-frame is a year, you may want to create monthly, bi-monthly or quarterly benchmarks. Remember, you not only can adjust your benchmarks as you reach them, but you actually should, because you may arrive at a benchmark slightly before or after your initial idea of where you will be. It is perfectly acceptable to overestimate or underestimate your benchmark, so either way, don't feel discouraged, just adjust your benchmark as necessary.

Step 3: Break Down Your Milestones

You want to concentrate just on your first benchmark until you have completed it. Figure out exactly what it will take to accomplish your goal and then create a weekly checklist (not all at once, but each week) to accomplish your first benchmarks. If you want to weigh a certain amount, increase your income by a certain amount, or any other goal that you happen to have, figure out what it will take to reach it and divide it up equally by the time that you have to reach that benchmark. Those are your weekly checklist items, and it is the foundation of your whole plan.

Step 4: Eliminate Distractions

Make your goal time a priority and don't allow any of the usual distractions during this time. They can pervade your life and waste your time any other point of your day or week, but never let distractions keep you from achieving the items that you have on your weekly (or monthly) checklist.

Step 5: Feel The Fear But Do It Anyway

You're going to have fears as you accomplish your goals, and you're going to have them the entire time, but you need to ignore them, because they aren't usually telling you anything useful or even true. You've been letting fear control you for so long, that it can be difficult to shut out those voices, but once you have accomplished some of your benchmarks you will notice that you don't even hear them anymore.

Step 6: Beat Procrastination In 5 Stages

You cannot put off until tomorrow what you can do today. You want to know why? Because that is exactly what you have been doing your entire life and you have obviously not accomplished everything that you want to. Stop procrastinating and get your weekly checklist items done. You'll feel great after you accomplish them, and you'll feel incredible once you have reached a few benchmarks or reached your final goal.

Procrastination has no place in the life of a successful person, and so when you find yourself procrastinating, put a stop to it immediately. Also, make an unbreakable rule that you will never procrastinate more than twice a week. If you do that, you should have no problem accomplishing your checklist items.

Step 7: Get And Stay Motivated

Use the techniques in chapter seven or anything else that helps you stay motivated. There are some good things in that chapter, but you can probably find even more with a little research. Staying motivated and doing all of your checklist items is the key to reaching your end goal.

My Final Words

So, there you go. A foolproof plan on how to stop procrastinating, stop letting distractions keep you from reaching your goals and getting things done.

Simply put, a journey of a thousands miles begins with the first step. All you need to do now is get started.

You now have a system you can follow along to beat procrastination and start achieving your goals.

IMPORTANT: To help you further take action, print out a copy of the *Checklist* and *Mindmap* I provided. You'll also find a Resource Cheat Sheet with valuable sites, posts and articles that I recommend you go through.

So, don't put it off. Let's get going on those goals right now, and don't forget – *Never Say Later!*

Printed by Libri Plureos GmbH in Hamburg,
Germany